D1090651

PIONEERS

OF THE

INDUSTRIAL AGE

BREAKTHROUGHS IN TECHNOLOGY

PIONEERS

OF THE

INDUSTRIAL

AGE

BREAKTHROUGHS IN TECHNOLOGY

Britannica
Educational Publishing
IN ASSOCIATION WITH

ROSEN
EDUCATIONAL SERVICES

EDITED BY
SHERMAN HOLLAR

609.2
P10

Published in 2013 by Britannica Educational Publishing
(a trademark of Encyclopædia Britannica, Inc.)
in association with Rosen Educational Services, LLC
29 East 21st Street, New York, NY 10010.

Copyright © 2013 Encyclopædia Britannica, Inc. Britannica, Encyclopædia Britannica, and the
Thistle logo are registered trademarks of Encyclopædia Britannica, Inc. All rights reserved.

Rosen Educational Services materials copyright © 2013 Rosen Educational Services, LLC.
All rights reserved.

Distributed exclusively by Rosen Educational Services.
For a listing of additional Britannica Educational Publishing titles, call toll free (800) 237-9932.

First Edition

Britannica Educational Publishing
J.E. Luebering: Director, Core Reference Group, Encyclopædia Britannica
Adam Augustyn: Assistant Manager, Encyclopædia Britannica

Anthony L. Green: Editor, Compton's by Britannica
Michael Anderson: Senior Editor, Compton's by Britannica
Andrea R. Field: Senior Editor, Compton's by Britannica
Sherman Hollar: Senior Editor, Compton's by Britannica

Marilyn L. Barton: Senior Coordinator, Production Control
Steven Bosco: Director, Editorial Technologies
Lisa S. Braucher: Senior Producer and Data Editor
Yvette Charboneau: Senior Copy Editor
Kathy Nakamura: Manager, Media Acquisition

Rosen Educational Services
Nicholas Croce: Rosen Editor
Nelson Sá: Art Director
Cindy Reiman: Photography Manager
Brian Garvey: Designer, Cover Design
Introduction by Nicholas Croce

Library of Congress Cataloging-in-Publication Data

Pioneers of the Industrial Age: breakthroughs in technology/edited by Sherman Hollar.—1st ed.
     p. cm.—(Inventors and innovators)
In association with Britannica Educational Publishing, Rosen Educational Services.
Includes bibliographical references and index.
ISBN 978-1-61530-696-1 (library binding)
1. Inventors—Biography—Popular works. 2. Inventions—History—Popular works.
I. Hollar, Sherman.
T39.P55 2013
609.2'2—dc23

                                                                                    2012005541

Manufactured in the United States of America

Cover, p. 3 © iStockphoto.com/Mark Goddard; interior background image © iStockphoto.com/
pialhovik

CONTENTS

INTRODUCTION

Orville and Wilbur Wright's first successful flight, on Dec. 17, 1903, at Kitty Hawk, NC.
Library of Congress Prints and Photographs Division

Though the Industrial Age began more than two centuries ago, we continue to benefit from it today. Every time one picks up an iPad, travels in an automobile, or text messages a friend, he or she can thank the pioneers of this transformative era in the history of invention, which created dramatic new means of production and brought about great technical advances in transportation and communication, among numerous other fields.

Many historians have come to view the process of industrialization as having occurred in two major periods: the First Industrial Revolution, which spanned from as early as 1760 to the mid-19th century, and the Second Industrial Revolution, which took place in the late 19th and 20th centuries. The First Industrial Revolution was mainly confined to Britain, Belgium, and France, while the Second Revolution witnessed the rise of other industrial powers, most notably the United States.

During these periods, nations transformed from largely agrarian economies to ones dominated by industry and machine manufacture. Technological changes included the use of new basic materials such as iron and steel and new energy sources such as coal, steam, electricity, and petroleum. These new technologies led to greater productivity, as in the example of the spinning jenny, a power loom created by English inventor James Hargreaves, which enabled workers to manufacture cloth with much greater efficiency.

Yet it wasn't just the technology itself but also manufacturing systems that increased productivity. The factory system allowed enterprises to better distribute tasks in the production process and to eliminate unnecessary work. In addition, developments in transportation technology, including the advent of steam-powered locomotives, steamships, automobiles, and airplanes, allowed for the mass distribution of the products that were created.

With new technologies and improved productivity came socioeconomic changes as well, including a wider distribution of wealth and increased international trade. The transition from an agrarian to an industrial society inspired the growth of cities and the working classes that inhabited them. The socioeconomic changes naturally fostered cultural shifts with workers abandoning the artisanal skills of the craftsman for those that involved operating machinery and working in a factory. Industrialization also brought about a psychological change as the increased capabilities of machines helped inspire a new confidence in society's ability to master nature by utilizing resources more efficiently.

This volume profiles some of the greatest innovators of the Industrial Age. Many are widely known for their contributions, such as Eli Whitney, inventor of the cotton gin; Samuel Morse, developer of the electric telegraph and Morse code; Alexander Graham Bell, the father of the electric telephone; Thomas Alva Edison, inventor of the phonograph and the incandescent lightbulb; and the Wright Brothers, pioneers of aviation. Others may not be as recognizable but they are no less influential. These include Guglielmo Marconi, inventor of a successful wireless telegraph; Edmund Cartwright, developer of the power loom for weaving; and Robert Fulton, the inventor who brought steamboating from the experimental stage to commercial success.

These pioneers, in their own way, helped forge the industrialized world and lay the foundation for the important breakthroughs to come.

CHAPTER 1

JOHN KAY

The 18th-century English machinist and engineer John Kay invented the flying shuttle, which was an important step toward automatic weaving. This device, one of the first breakthroughs of the Industrial Revolution, transformed the textile industry.

Kay, the son of a wool manufacturer, was born near the town of Bury in Lancashire, Eng., on July 16, 1704. His father placed young John in charge of the family mill, and the youth took advantage of this opportunity by making several improvements to the mill's machinery.

In 1733 Kay received a patent for a "New Engine or Machine for Opening and Dressing Wool" that used his ingenious flying shuttle. In previous looms, the shuttle was passed through the lengthwise, or warp, threads by hand, and wide fabrics required two weavers seated side by side passing the shuttle from left to right and then back again. Kay mounted the shuttle on wheels in a track and used paddles to

John Kay. Science & Society Picture Library/Getty Images

shoot the shuttle from side to side when the weaver jerked a cord. Using a flying shuttle, one weaver could weave cloth of any width more quickly than two could before.

Wool manufacturers throughout Yorkshire quickly adopted the new invention, but they also organized a protective club to avoid paying Kay a royalty. Desperate to protect his patent, Kay spent most of his money on legal fees. He also faced a problem with weavers, who considered the flying shuttle a menace to labor and destroyed a model of the device. Kay moved to France and resumed his work, but he is said to have died in obscurity, probably in 1764. Kay's invention so increased yarn consumption that it spurred the invention of spinning machines, but its true importance lay in its adaptation in power looms.

CHAPTER 2

JAMES HARGREAVES

The obscurity of James Hargreaves's life contrasts sharply with the worldwide influence of his invention, a yarn-spinning machine called the spinning jenny. Relatively little is known of his life. He was baptized on Jan. 8, 1721, in Oswaldtwistle in Lancashire, Eng. While still a boy, he became a carpenter and spinner in Standhill, a village nearby. At that time Lancashire was the center of England's manufacture of cotton goods. The industry was still confined to workers' homes, however, and the cards, spinning wheels, and looms were operated by hand.

It is said that an accident gave Hargreaves the idea for his spinning jenny. In his crowded cottage, which served him both as home and workshop, he was experimenting with spinning two threads at one time. His experiments were unsuccessful, however, because the horizontal spindles allowed the threads to fly apart and become tangled. After his daughter Jenny overturned

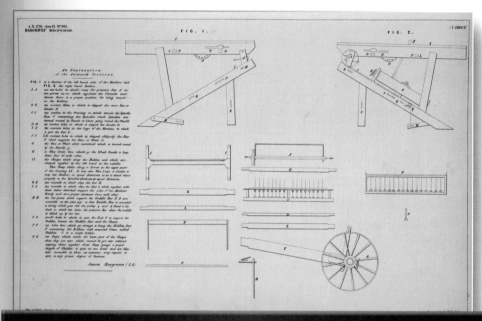

1770 patent drawing of the spinning jenny. Science & Society Picture Library/Getty Images

the experimental machine and its wheel continued to revolve with the spindles in a vertical position, it occurred to Hargreaves that a machine with spindles in this position might be successful. He proceeded to build a spinning machine, probably in 1764, that would spin eight threads at the same time. He called his new invention a spinning jenny.

The amount of cotton yarn he and his children began to produce alarmed other spinners, who feared that the machine would put them out of work; so they broke into his home and destroyed his machine. In 1768 he moved to the town of Nottingham, where he set up a fairly profitable yarn mill to supply hosiers. In 1770 he patented the spinning jenny. Since he had sold several of his machines, the patent was declared invalid when challenged in court. This left others free to use the invention without paying him royalties.

Before Hargreaves's death on April 22, 1778, in Nottinghamshire, mechanical spinning was fully developed by Richard Arkwright and Samuel Crompton. Later Edmund Cartwright invented the mechanical loom.

CHAPTER 3

RICHARD ARKWRIGHT

The father of the modern industrial factory system was Richard Arkwright. A self-educated man, he invented many machines for mass-producing yarn and was responsible for establishing cotton-cloth manufacture as the leading industry in northern England.

Richard Arkwright was born on Dec. 23, 1732, in Preston, Eng., a seaport town. He was the youngest of 13 children of a poor laboring man. Apprenticed to a barber in Bolton, Arkwright married in 1755. After the death of his first wife, Patience Holt, by whom he had a son, he married Margaret Biggins in 1761. Margaret had a small income, which enabled Arkwright to expand his barbering business. He acquired a secret method for dyeing hair and traveled about the country purchasing human hair for use in the manufacture of wigs. His travels brought him into contact with people who were concerned with weaving and spinning. When the fashion for wearing wigs declined, he looked to mechanical inventions in the field of textiles to make his fortune.

By 1767 a machine for carding cotton had been introduced into England, and James Hargreaves had invented the spinning jenny. These machines called for considerable hand labor, however, and Hargreaves's jenny produced inferior yarn. With the help of a clockmaker, Arkwright constructed a spinning machine that produced a stronger yarn. He then built his first spinning mill.

Arkwright's horse-driven spinning mill at Preston was the first of his many mills. By 1775 he had developed mills in which the whole process of yarn manufacture was carried on by one machine. His system of division of factory labor is still used today. He was also the first to use James Watt's steam engine to power textile machinery, though he used it only to pump water to the mill-race of a waterwheel. From

Richard Arkwright's original carding machine. Hulton Archive/Getty Images

the combined use of the steam engine and the machinery, the power loom eventually was developed.

Arkwright's patents were attacked and declared void in 1785, largely as a result of testimony by the clockmaker. His machinery was widely copied by other manufacturers. Arkwright was knighted by George III in 1786. For several years he was able to fix the price of cotton yarn in England, and he was able to leave a large fortune at his death, in Cromford, on Aug. 3, 1792.

CHAPTER 4

JAMES WATT

It is sometimes said that James Watt got the idea for a steam engine while still a boy, watching steam lift the lid of his mother's teakettle. The truth is that Watt did not invent the steam engine; however, he made major improvements on the inefficient steam engine of his time.

James Watt was born in Greenock, Sco., on Jan. 19, 1736. His father ran a successful ship- and house-building business. He apprenticed to an instrument maker in London in 1755. In 1767 he became instrument maker for the University of Glasgow, where he developed his lifelong interest in steam engines.

For more than a century, inventors had tried to use steam power for pumping water from England's coal mines. The best result in Watt's time was an inefficient engine patented in 1705 by Thomas Newcomen, John Cawley, and Thomas Savery.

Watt was given the opportunity to improve on this slow and wasteful engine

James Watt. Science & Society Picture Library/Getty Images

when the university's model needed repair in 1764. One improvement gained speed by making the engine double-acting. Watt did this with valves that admitted steam to each side of the piston in turn. At each admission to one side, the valves released the steam on the other side to a separate vessel, where it was condensed. This avoided chilling the cylinder at each stroke, and the condensation created a vacuum that made the new steam more effective. Watt obtained his first patent in 1769.

Watt's engine was very successful in pumping. For turning wheels in factories, however, it needed some device for changing the back-and-forth motion of the piston into rotary motion. So Watt made the piston drive a connecting rod and a crank that turned an axle. A former employee patented the crank, and Watt had to use less adequate methods for securing circular motion until the patent expired in 1781.

Watt immigrated to Birmingham, Eng., in 1774. There he won the support of the manufacturer Matthew Boulton, and in 1775 the two men formed a partnership that would last 25 years. The financial support that

Boulton was able to provide made possible rapid progress with the engine.

Watt never developed engines that were powerful for their weight, because he refused to use high-pressure steam. Another improvement, however, was his steam governor. The governor used two heavy balls, mounted on swinging arms. The arms were connected to regulate the steam valve. The whole assembly was geared to rotate with the engine's motion. It also maintained the motion at a desired speed. If the engine sped up, centrifugal force drove the balls outward in wider circles. This moved the arms. The arms choked the steam valve, thereby reducing speed. If the engine lagged, the balls lowered and admitted more steam. By 1790 Watt had earned enough money to let him retire to his estate near Birmingham, where he died on Aug. 25, 1819.

CHAPTER 5

EDMUND CARTWRIGHT

The Industrial Revolution started in Great Britain during the 18th century largely with the mechanization of the textile industry. One of the men who made significant contributions to this mechanization was a clergyman-turned-inventor named Edmund Cartwright, who devised the power loom for weaving.

Cartwright was born in Marnham in Nottinghamshire on April 24, 1743. He was educated at Wakefield grammar school and Oxford University. In 1779 he became the rector of the parish of Goadby Marwood in Leicestershire. He would probably have passed his life as an obscure country clergyman but for a visit to Cromford in 1784. There he saw Richard Arkwright's cotton-spinning mills. These fascinated him, and he decided to construct a similar machine for weaving. In 1785 he took out a patent for a very simple machine. It was later

Edmund Cartwright. Science & Society Picture Library/Getty Images

improved and developed into the modern power loom.

Also in 1785 Cartwright opened a weaving and spinning factory in Doncaster. The business failed by 1793. Another misfortune was a fire that destroyed a mill in Manchester where a number of his machines had been installed. In 1789 he patented a wool-combing machine. It lowered manufacturing costs, but he made little money from it or from any of his inventions.

In 1809 the British Parliament, in recognition of the benefits bestowed on the nation through the power loom, voted to award Cartwright a payment of £10,000. He bought a farm in Hollander, where he spent many years. He also invented a rope-making machine, a steam engine that operated on alcohol, and various farm implements. He died in Hastings on Oct. 30, 1823.

CHAPTER 6

SAMUEL CROMPTON

The inventor of the spinning mule for yarn making, Samuel Crompton helped revolutionize the English textile industry. His improvements of the machines made by Hargreaves and Arkwright transformed spinning from a hand-operated cottage industry to the machine-operated factory process of today.

Samuel Crompton was born in Lancashire, Eng., on Dec. 3, 1753. His father died when the boy was 16 years old, and he went to work as a yarn spinner to support the family. He inherited ambition and perseverance from his mother, and after working all day he tramped to Bolton to attend night school.

The yarn produced by Hargreaves's spinning jenny was too coarse and rough for fine grades of cloth, and young Crompton set about the task of overcoming these defects. For ten years he earned a scanty living by

Samuel Crompton's spinning mule frame. Science & Society Picture Library/Getty Images

day, and by night worked at his invention, which he was obliged to guard from his suspicious neighbors. With no money to pay the fees for a patent or for legal advice, he was cheated out of his rights by manufacturers with whom he made contracts for the use of his invention.

It was 20 years before Crompton had the means to set up a small factory in Bolton, and by that time thousands of his spinning machines were in use, with no profit for him. He called his machine the "spinning mule," because it was a hybrid combining the principles of Hargreaves's jenny and Arkwright's roller frame. It produced a finer, smoother, and more elastic yarn, so Crompton's invention in the end displaced the other. With minor improvements it is used in every textile mill in the world today. Yet all his life this genius, who had made wealth for many lesser men, was poor. In 1812 Parliament belatedly granted him £5,000 which was lost in unlucky business ventures. He died on June 26, 1827.

CHAPTER 7

ROBERT FULTON

The man who did the most to make steamboats a commercial success was Robert Fulton. Other inventors pioneered in steam navigation before him, but it was Fulton who proved that their vision and designs were practical.

Robert Fulton was born on Nov. 14, 1765, on a Pennsylvania farm in what is now Fulton Township. At 17 he went to Philadelphia to work for a jeweler and to study art. He used his talents so well that at 21 he had $400 to invest in a farm for his widowed mother and sisters. He then went to London to study art with the well-known painter Benjamin West.

In England he made friends in the scientific and engineering fields. Soon his interest in art was forgotten in the midst of his work on a series of inventions, including dredging machines, flax-spinning and rope-making devices, and a substitute for canal locks.

In 1797 he proposed the building of a submarine to the French government. It

Robert Fulton. Stock Montage/Archive Photos/Getty Images

rejected his idea, but Fulton eventually built and launched *Nautilus* on his own in 1800. In Paris in 1801 he met the American minister Robert R. Livingston, who had obtained a 20-year monopoly on steamboat navigation in the state of New York. He returned to the United States as Livingston's partner to work out a practical steamboat, using an engine and boiler purchased in England from Boulton & Watt. On Aug. 17, 1807, Fulton's first steamboat, the *Clermont*, made a trial voyage—from New York Harbor, up the Hudson River, to Albany and back. The experiment was a triumph, discrediting skeptics who had called it "Fulton's folly." During the next eight years Fulton established and managed steamboat lines, and in 1814 he was commissioned by the federal government to build its first steam warship. He died in New York City on Feb. 24, 1815.

CHAPTER 8

ELI WHITNEY

Best remembered as the inventor of the cotton gin, Eli Whitney also developed the concept of mass production of interchangeable parts and the assembly line.

Whitney was born in Westboro, Mass., on Dec. 8, 1765. As a boy he became skilled as a mechanic in a farm workshop. After graduating from Yale College in 1792, he went to Savannah, Ga., where he learned of the major problem of the South: how to produce enough cotton to meet the demands of England's newly invented spinning and weaving machines. A black-seed, long-staple cotton was easily cleaned, but it grew only near the coast, while a green-seed, short-staple variety grew in inland areas but resisted cleaning since its fiber stuck to the seed. Whitney resolved to invent a machine to clean the green-seed cotton.

Never having seen raw cotton, Whitney realized that comblike teeth of some sort were necessary. Within days he had a crude model. Based on simple principles, the

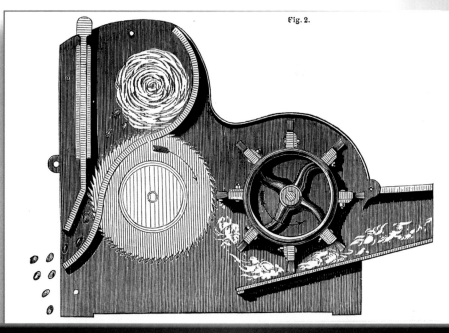

Fig. 2.

Cross-section of Eli Whitney's cotton gin. © Image Asset Management Ltd./SuperStock

cotton gin was finished in 1793. By 1800 cotton production had increased from about 3,000 bales a year to 73,000. His cotton-cleaning invention brought prosperity to the South.

Whitney patented the gin in 1794 and formed a business partnership with Phineas Miller. The unwillingness of planters to pay for the rights to use the gin brought many lawsuits. Whitney's machine was copied, his patent was infringed, and his factory was set on fire. Defending his rights in court used up Whitney's earnings. Heavily in debt in 1798, Whitney contracted with the United States government to make 10,000 muskets. Until then guns had been hand-made; no two were alike. Whitney designed a new gun and the machinery to make it. His machine manufactured parts exactly alike. Each part would fit any of the guns he made. Whitney also created division of labor, in which each person specialized in making one part of the gun. The final step was merely to assemble the interchangeable parts. Whitney died in New Haven, Conn., on Jan. 8, 1825.

CHAPTER 9

SAMUEL SLATER

The founder of the American cotton textile industry was an English immigrant named Samuel Slater. Because of his mechanical knowledge and ability as an inventor, he was forced to leave England secretly. At that time skilled mechanics were forbidden to emigrate.

Slater was born on June 9, 1768, in Belper, Derbyshire. In 1783 he became an apprentice in a factory that made textile machinery. He was eventually promoted to supervisor of machinery. When he heard about the need for skilled mechanics in the United States he left England in 1789. He went to work for the Almy and Brown textile firm in Providence, R.I., and redesigned their equipment in accordance with English specifications. He reproduced the designs of Richard Arkwright, who had invented the spinning frame. Slater had carried all of the designs to the United States in his head, not daring to write them down before he emigrated for fear of being discovered. The

Samuel Slater. Hulton Archive/Getty Images

mill he designed was finished and put into service in 1793, and his name was included in that of the firm.

Slater's wife developed a way of making high-quality cotton thread. To manufacture it Slater founded Samuel Slater and Company in 1798. He later joined other family members in starting a textile plant in Pawtucket, R.I. By 1812 he controlled 12 manufacturing plants in New England. He also gave freely of his time as a consultant to other industrialists. Slater remained active in the textile business until his death on April 21, 1835, in Webster, Mass.

CHAPTER 10

THE STEPHENSON FAMILY

Among the outstanding figures in the history of the railroad were three members of the Stephenson family. The English engineer George Stephenson, principal inventor of the railroad locomotive; his son Robert, a master engineer known for the innovative design of his bridges; and George's nephew George Robert cooperated to build some of the first railroads in the world.

GEORGE STEPHENSON

George Stephenson was born on June 9, 1781, in the mining village of Wylam, Northumberland, Eng. He went to work at an early age and without formal schooling. In 1814 he built the *Blucher*, one of the first railroad locomotives. In 1815 he patented an engine with a steam blast, by which exhaust steam was redirected up the chimney. The new design increased the engine's power and rendered the locomotive truly practical. In the same year Stephenson also invented a safety lamp for miners.

In 1822 he was commissioned to build a steam locomotive for a railroad line to be built from Stockton to Darlington. His son, Robert, assisted him in survey work for the tracks, and on Sept. 27, 1825, railroad transportation was born.

In 1823 George Stephenson established a locomotive works in Newcastle. George and Robert then cooperated in the construction of a railway connecting Liverpool and Manchester. In 1829 the railway company held a competition to find a suitable locomotive for the line; George and Robert won the contest with the *Rocket*, an engine with a multi-tubular boiler. George Stephenson died in Chesterfield, Derbyshire, on Aug. 12, 1848.

ROBERT STEPHENSON

Robert Stephenson was George's only son. He was born in Willington Quay, Northumberland, on Oct. 16, 1803. He studied mathematics at Bruce's Academy in Newcastle upon Tyne and later attended

Robert Stephenson. Science & Society Picture Library/Getty Images

Edinburgh University. He managed the Newcastle locomotive works and in 1833 was appointed chief engineer of the London and Birmingham Railway, the first railway into London. He directed several major engineering works, but he is best known for his long-span railroad bridges. Robert died in London on Oct. 12, 1859.

GEORGE ROBERT STEPHENSON

George Robert Stephenson was born on Oct. 20, 1819, in Newcastle upon Tyne, Northumberland. A civil engineer educated at King William College on the Isle of Man, he entered his uncle George Stephenson's employ in 1837 during the construction of a railway from Manchester to Leeds. He helped Robert build the Victoria tubular bridge across the St. Lawrence River in Canada and served as a consultant and designer on independent projects in England and abroad. Upon Robert's death in 1859, he became director of the Newcastle locomotive works. George Robert died on Oct. 26, 1905, in Cheltenham, Gloucestershire.

CHAPTER 11

SAMUEL F.B. MORSE

"I wish that in one instant I could tell you of my safe arrival, but we are 3,000 miles apart and must wait four long weeks to hear from each other." Samuel Morse was 20 when he wrote this sentence in a letter to his mother in 1811. He was in London studying art. She was at the home in Charlestown, Mass., where he had been born. Perhaps it was at the moment of writing the letter that young Morse first conceived the desire to bridge space with flying words. This desire was later to give the world the electric telegraph.

Samuel Finley Breese Morse was born on April 27, 1791. He was the eldest son of Jedidiah Morse, a noted Congregational minister, and Elizabeth Ann Breese Morse. He was educated at Phillips Academy, in Andover, and at Yale University. While he was in college he became interested in electricity, but his chief enthusiasm was art. His father opposed a career as an artist. He sent him to London to study art in 1811, however, after Gilbert Stuart praised his work.

Samuel F.B. Morse standing with the telegraph he developed in the 1830s, photograph by Mathew Brady. Library of Congress, Washington, D.C.

When Samuel returned in 1815 he found, however, that Americans were not interested in buying paintings—even paintings that had hung in the Royal Academy. He made a meager living painting portraits. The best known were two of the Marquis de Lafayette, painted in 1825. Morse's dramatic personality and brilliant conversation won him a place of leadership in New York's artistic and intellectual circles. He helped to found the National Academy of Design and was its president. After 1835 he held a professorship in art at the University of the City of New York.

Morse was inspired to invent the telegraph by a chance conversation while returning from Europe on the steamship *Sully* in 1832. A fellow passenger told him about European experiments in electromagnetism. Morse remarked: "If the presence of electricity can be made visible in any part of the circuit, I see no reason why intelligence may not be transmitted by electricity." During the rest of the voyage he worked excitedly on drawings for his plan.

Morse had an inventive mind but little knowledge of electricity. Years of work and study were needed to perfect his device. People admired his determination in the face of poverty and disappointment. He received practical help from industrialist Alfred Vail, physicist Joseph Henry, and others. In 1837 he applied for a patent on the American Electromagnetic Telegraph. He went to England, France, and Russia seeking aid for his invention but met with failure there as at home. Finally in 1843 the United States Congress appropriated $30,000 to build a line from Washington to Baltimore. In May 1844 the first message was flashed over this wire. Its text was: "What hath God wrought?"

After his years of sacrifice, Morse enjoyed to the fullest the wealth and honors that came to him as a great inventor. Newspapers, railroads, and businesses quickly found use for the telegraph. After the founding of Western Union in 1856, wires were soon strung from coast to coast. Other men of science had worked on the problem, but Morse's invention was the basis of the land telegraph systems that developed. The code of dots and dashes used in sending messages is still known as the Morse code in honor of its inventor. He worked as the electrician in Cyrus W. Field's first attempt to lay a cable across the Atlantic Ocean in 1857. Morse resigned, predicting the initial failure that soon followed. The inventor's estate, Locust Grove, on the Hudson River was noted for its gatherings of distinguished people. Morse became a leader in cultural and civic affairs. When he died in 1872, on April 2, public memorial meetings were held across the nation.

CHAPTER 12

CHARLES GOODYEAR

Charles Goodyear invented the vulcanization process that made possible the commercial use of rubber. He was born in New Haven, Conn., on Dec. 29, 1800. Goodyear began his career as a partner in his father's hardware business, which went bankrupt in 1830. He then became interested in discovering a method of treating India rubber so that it would lose its adhesiveness and susceptibility to extremes of heat and cold. He developed a nitric acid treatment and in 1837 contracted for the manufacture by this process of mailbags for the U.S. government, but the rubber fabric proved useless at high temperatures.

For the next few years he worked with a former employee of a rubber factory who had discovered that rubber treated with sulfur was not sticky. Goodyear bought the process, and in 1839 he accidentally dropped some India rubber mixed with sulfur on a hot stove and so discovered vulcanization. He was granted his first patent

Charles Goodyear. Hulton Archive/Getty Images

in 1844 but had to fight numerous infringements in court; the decisive victory did not come until 1852. That year he went to England, where articles made under his patents had been displayed at the International Exhibition of 1851; while there he unsuccessfully attempted to establish factories. He also lost his patent rights there and in France because of technical and legal problems. In France a company that manufactured vulcanized rubber by his process failed, and in December 1855 Goodyear was imprisoned for debt in Paris. Meanwhile, in the United States, his patents continued to be infringed upon. Although his invention made millions for others, at his death in New York City on July 1, 1860, he left debts of some $200,000. He wrote an account of his discovery entitled *Gum-Elastic and Its Varieties* (1853–55). The Goodyear Tire & Rubber Company was named in his honor, though neither he nor his family were connected to the business.

CHAPTER 13

CYRUS HALL McCORMICK

Responsible in large part for liberating farmworkers from hours of backbreaking labor, Cyrus Hall McCormick introduced his newly invented reaper in July 1831. That month a crowd gathered near the town of Steele's Tavern, Va., and waited skeptically as McCormick prepared to demonstrate his strange-looking machine. To their amazement the machine cut the grain faster than they could do it with their cradle scythes.

McCormick was born on his family's farm at Walnut Grove in Rockbridge County, Va., on Feb. 15, 1809. His father, a prosperous landowner, had a keen interest in the mechanical side of farm life. When his father abandoned his efforts to build a reaper, young McCormick began to work on a machine of his own.

For years people had been experimenting with mechanical reapers. Some inventions had already been patented in England and

Cyrus Hall McCormick. Fotosearch/Archive Photos/Getty Images

the United States. Obed Hussey in Cincinnati, Ohio, developed a model that he patented in 1833. Six months later, in 1834, McCormick patented his improved reaper.

After the patent was granted he continued to work on improvements. In 1840 he sold his first two machines in Virginia. In 1847 he built a manufacturing plant in

Chicago, Ill., in the heart of the new grain-growing section of the Middle West.

McCormick soon began manufacturing on a large scale, advertising, demonstrating, and guaranteeing his product, offering replaceable parts, and selling on the installment plan. In spite of lawsuits and competition, he was for years the dominant figure in the industry. When the Civil War broke out, the 50,000 reapers then being used released thousands of men for duty at the front. His machine also won recognition abroad—in England in 1851 and finally throughout the world. McCormick died in Chicago on May 13, 1884.

By 1875 the McCormick factories were turning out thousands of reapers and mowers every year. Before the end of the century, they had introduced scores of other tools to speed farmwork and lessen its drudgery.

CHAPTER 14

ELIAS HOWE

Before Elias Howe invented the sewing machine, the fastest sewing possible was only about 50 stitches per minute. Howe's invention stitched five times faster than that. It eventually helped to establish mass production of clothing and other sewn goods.

Elias Howe was born in Spencer, Mass., on July 9, 1819. While still small, he worked on his father's farm and gristmill. When he was 16 he went to Lowell, where he worked in a factory making cotton-weaving machinery, and he later moved to Cambridge. He married in 1841.

Around the same year, Howe heard of the need for a machine that could sew. The problem fascinated him, and he spent all his spare time during the next five years developing a practical sewing machine. First he tried using a needle that was pointed at both ends, with an eye in the middle. It was a failure. Then he conceived of a machine that made a lockstitch. Howe left his job to

The first Elias Howe sewing machine, from a wood engraving. © Photos.com/Jupiterimages

work on his invention. Unable to support his wife and three children, he decided to move them into his father's home. Shortly thereafter he interested a friend, George Fisher, in his machine. Fisher invited the Howe family into his home and gave Howe money to continue with his work. Howe completed his first successful sewing machine in 1845.

In 1846 Howe was granted a patent for his invention. The machine was ill received in the United States because people feared it might displace those employed in hand sewing. Howe sold the English rights for about $1,250. He then went to London to adapt the machine to the buyer's special needs, but his salary was small, and he later returned to the United States destitute. Upon his arrival, he found his wife dying. While he had been abroad, sewing machines were being widely manufactured and sold in the United States in flagrant violation of his patent. After much litigation, his rights were finally established in 1854. From then until the time that his patent expired, he received royalties on all sewing machines produced in the country. Howe died on Oct. 3, 1867, in Brooklyn, N.Y.

CHAPTER 15

ANDREW CARNEGIE

The history of the industrialist and philanthropist Andrew Carnegie is one of the great American success stories. At 12 he was an immigrant boy earning $1.20 a week. Fifty years later he was giving away a third of a billion dollars of his own money. Meanwhile he had built up one of the world's largest steel companies.

Andrew Carnegie was born on Nov. 25, 1835, at Dunfermline near Edinburgh, Sco. In 1848 the family came to America, settling at Allegheny, Pa. (now part of Pittsburgh). Young Andrew worked first as a bobbin boy in a cotton mill. Later he became a messenger in a telegraph office and then secretary to the superintendent of the Pennsylvania Railroad's Pittsburgh division. By the outbreak of the Civil War he himself was superintendent. He had also become a financier. Saving his earnings, he bought an interest in a sleeping-car company. The stock increased greatly in value when United States railroads adopted

Andrew Carnegie. Ernest H. Mills/Hulton Archive/Getty Images

sleeping cars, and young Carnegie made a great deal of money.

During the war he gave up his position to take charge of the eastern military railroads and telegraph lines for the government. After the Civil War he could see that iron bridges would soon replace wooden structures. So he founded the Keystone Bridge Works, which built the first iron bridge across the Ohio River. This business led him to found the iron and steel works that brought him the bulk of his huge fortune.

By 1899 Carnegie had consolidated many of the steel works located around Pittsburgh into the Carnegie Steel Company. Two years later, at the height of his phenomenal business career, he transferred his $500-million steel interests to the new United States Steel Corporation. He then retired from business so that he could devote his time and money to public service.

Carnegie believed that it was the solemn duty of a rich man to redistribute his wealth in the public interest. He also felt, however, that indiscriminate giving was bad. "No person," he said, "and no community can be permanently helped except by their own cooperation."

To ensure that his money would be distributed wisely, he established the Carnegie Corporation of New York, with an endowment of $125 million. The income from this fund now goes to many causes. His biggest gift for any single purpose was the fund for establishing the Carnegie public libraries. Almost as famous are the Hero Funds he set up in many countries to recognize heroic acts that might otherwise go unappreciated.

Most of his fortune went to educational and scientific institutions. Many of these he founded himself. Among the other organizations were the Carnegie Endowment for International Peace, founded in 1910, and the Carnegie Foundation for the Advancement of Teaching, established in 1905.

Carnegie was devoted to his mother and supported her in luxurious fashion. He did not marry until after her death, when he was in his 50s. He and his wife bought a huge estate in Scotland and built a great house they called Skibo Castle. In his later years he was half-humorously known as the Laird of Skibo. Carnegie died at Shadowbrook, his summer home in Lenox, Mass., at the age of 83.

The first Carnegie Hero Fund Commission was established in Pittsburgh in 1904 with a grant of $5 million. Inscribed on the medal that its trustees award to persons who save—or attempt to save—the lives of others is the Biblical quotation, "Greater love hath no man than this, that a man lay down his life for his friends." Also in the philanthropist's memory, the Carnegie Medal has been awarded annually since 1937 for the best children's book published in Great Britain.

CHAPTER 16

MARGARET E. KNIGHT

Margaret E. Knight was a prolific inventor of machines and mechanisms for a variety of industrial and everyday purposes. Knight was born on Feb. 14, 1838, in York, Maine. She demonstrated a knack for tools and invention from an early age, and she was said to have contrived a safety device for controlling shuttles in powered textile looms when she was 12 years old. In 1868, at which time she was living in Springfield, Mass., she invented an attachment for paper-bag-folding machines that allowed the production of square-bottomed bags. After working to improve her invention in Boston, she patented it in 1870. She later received patents for a dress and skirt shield (1883), a clasp for robes (1884), and a spit (1885). Later still she received six patents over a span of years for machines used in the manufacturing of shoes.

Other of Knight's inventions included a numbering machine and a window frame and sash, both patented in 1894, and several devices relating to rotary engines, patented between 1902 and 1915. Although she was not the first woman to receive a patent, she was one of the most productive of female inventors, having some 27 patents to her credit. She failed to profit much from her work, however. After Knight died on Oct. 12, 1914, in Framingham, Mass., she was honored in a local obituary as a "woman Edison."

CHAPTER 17

JOHN D. ROCKEFELLER

John D. Rockefeller founded the Standard Oil Company, which dominated the oil industry and was the first great U.S. business trust. Rockefeller was born on July 8, 1839, in Richford, N.Y. He moved with his family to Ohio, where he completed his high school education. In 1863 Rockefeller built his first petroleum refinery near Cleveland, Ohio, after observing the commercial potential of oil production in western Pennsylvania. In 1870 Rockefeller, along with associates who included his older brother William, incorporated his petroleum holdings into the Standard Oil Company (Ohio). Rockefeller bought out his competitors or put them out of business through tactics that included price cutting and the acquisition of such supporting enterprises as pipelines, oil terminals, and cooperage plants. By 1881, when Rockefeller formed a trust with nine directors to control Standard Oil and its

John D. Rockefeller. Hulton Archive/Getty Images

affiliates, he had a near monopoly of the petroleum industry in the United States.

Public hostility against monopolies in general and against Standard Oil specifically led to the passage of the Sherman Anti-Trust Act (1890). In 1892 Rockefeller was forced to dissolve the trust. He then placed control of his properties in companies located in various states and in 1899 brought the companies together in a holding company—the Standard Oil Company (New Jersey). In 1911 the United States Supreme Court declared this illegal, and the properties were separated.

From 1897 Rockefeller had turned his interests toward philanthropy. He endowed the University of Chicago and ultimately gave the school more than $80 million. He endowed major philanthropic institutions, including the Rockefeller Institute for Medical Research (later Rockefeller University) in New York City (1901), the General Education Board (1902), the Rockefeller Foundation (1913), and the Laura Spelman Rockefeller Memorial Foundation (1918), named for his late wife. Rockefeller died on May 23, 1937, in Ormond Beach, Fla.

CHAPTER 18

ELIJAH MCCOY

Elijah McCoy was an inventor who devised automatic lubrication used in locomotives, steamships, and machinery. His standard of quality was so rigorous that the term "the real McCoy" came to be applied to his lubricators and to stand for the highest quality product available.

McCoy was born in about 1843 in Colchester, Ont. His parents had moved there from the U.S. state of Kentucky to escape slavery. McCoy became interested in how machines work at a young age. As a young man he studied mechanical engineering in Scotland. Later he moved to Michigan, where he went to work for the Michigan Central Railroad.

One of McCoy's first jobs involved lubricating the moving parts of the railroad cars. At the time this had to be done by hand. The train had to be stopped and then someone would have to walk around and add oil to all the different parts to keep them moving well. McCoy saw how this could

Elijah McCoy. Schomburg Center for Research in Black Culture/NYPL/Photo Researchers, Inc.

be done more easily. In 1872 he invented a device that would automatically add oil as it was needed and as the train kept moving. The device was extremely successful. He soon came up with several other inventions.

In time McCoy was able to stop working for the railroad and concentrate on creating new inventions. Most of those also had to do with lubricating machines. He received more than 50 patents for his work. McCoy died in Michigan in 1929.

CHAPTER 19

GEORGE WESTINGHOUSE

"If I understand you, young man, you propose to stop a railroad train with wind. I have no time to listen to such nonsense." Commodore Cornelius Vanderbilt, the powerful railroad owner, thus dismissed George Westinghouse and his new air brake. But within a few years the old hand brakes on trains were replaced with air brakes, launching Westinghouse into a notable career as inventor and industrialist.

Westinghouse was born on Oct. 6, 1846, in Central Bridge, N.Y. The son of a manufacturer of farm implements, he explored the world of machines at an early age. After serving in both the Union Army and the Navy in the Civil War, Westinghouse received in 1865 his first patent—for a rotary steam engine. In that same year he invented a device for replacing derailed freight cars on their tracks.

Railroad problems fascinated Westinghouse. Among his other inventions was a device called a frog that allowed wheels on

George Westinghouse. Library of Congress Prints and Photographs Division

one rail of a track to cross an intersecting rail. He bought various patents on railroad switches and signals and combined them with his own developments into an efficient switching system. He also devised safe methods to distribute natural gas.

The air brake, his greatest invention, was patented in 1869, the same year he organized the Westinghouse Air Brake Company. With various design improvements, the air brake became widely accepted, and the Railroad Safety Appliance Act of 1893 made them compulsory on trains in the United States.

Westinghouse was chiefly responsible for the adoption of alternating current (AC) systems for electric power transmission in the United States, which up to the 1880s had used direct current (DC) systems. Importing an AC system from Europe, Westinghouse purchased the patents of Nikola Tesla's AC motor and hired him to improve and modify the motor for use in the power system (see Tesla). Once the new system was ready, advocates of DC power set out to discredit AC power. Public acceptance of AC power came soon after Westinghouse dramatically proved its advantages at the World's Columbian Exposition in Chicago (1893).

Using incandescent and arc lighting, the fairground was set aglow with light. With buildings set like jewels against the evening sky, the display marked the start of large-scale outdoor lighting and of illuminated advertising signs.

Most of the Westinghouse factories were located in the Pittsburgh, Pa., area, and associated companies were established throughout the world. Westinghouse lost most of his control over his industrial empire during the financial panic of 1907. He died in New York City on March 12, 1914.

CHAPTER 20

ALEXANDER GRAHAM BELL

Other people before Bell had tried to transmit the human voice across distances. Others since have helped improve and perfect Bell's inventions. But Alexander Graham Bell will always be remembered as the father of the electric telephone.

Bell was born in Edinburgh, Sco., on March 3, 1847. He was educated at Edinburgh University and University College, London. With his parents, he moved to Brantford, Ont., in 1870. His father and grandfather had devoted their lives to the study of human speech and to teaching the deaf to speak, and he followed their profession. His main interest throughout his life was in helping the deaf.

In 1871 Bell started teaching deaf pupils in Boston. The following year he opened a private school to train teachers of the deaf in the methods of visible speech, which had been devised by his father. He began teaching at Boston University in 1873. In July 1877 he married Mabel Hubbard, one of his pupils.

Alexander Graham Bell shows how the telephone uses electricity to transmit sound over great distances, at a demonstration in Massachusetts in 1887. Library of Congress, Washington, D.C

In 1874–75 he began work on his great invention, inspired by experiments with devices to help the deaf. On March 10, 1876, in Boston, the first sentence was successfully transmitted by telephone. The historic words were spoken to his assistant, Thomas Watson: "Mr. Watson, come here; I want you."

Bell's attorney had applied for a patent on February 14 of that year, just two hours before Elisha Gray filed a notice in the Patent Office covering some of the same principles. At the Centennial Exposition of 1876, in Philadelphia, Pa., the demonstrations of Bell's remarkable telephone made a great sensation among the general public. Bell helped found the magazine *Science* in 1880.

In 1880 Bell received the French government's Volta prize of 50,000 francs for his invention of the telephone. He used the money to establish the Volta Laboratory and the American Association to Promote the Teaching of Speech to the Deaf in Washington, D.C. The association's name was changed to the Alexander Graham Bell Association for the Deaf in 1956. It is an international information center for the oral education of the deaf.

In 1898 Bell succeeded his father-in-law as president of the National Geographic Society. Convinced that geography could be taught through pictures, Bell sought to promote an understanding of life in distant lands in an era when only the privileged could travel. He was aided by his future son-in-law, Gilbert Grosvenor, who transformed what had begun as a modest pamphlet into a unique educational journal—*National Geographic Magazine*.

Among Bell's other inventions was an audiometer, for measuring the intensity of sound. He also experimented in aviation. His wife founded the Aerial Experiment Association—the first research organization established by a woman.

For many years Bell spent his summers at his estate on Cape Breton Island in Nova Scotia. He died there on Aug. 2, 1922. During the funeral service every telephone of the Bell system was kept silent. In 1950 Bell was elected to the Hall of Fame at New York University.

CHAPTER 21

THOMAS ALVA EDISON

When he was 21 years old, Thomas Edison took out his first patent. It was for an electric vote counter to be used in the United States House of Representatives. The machine worked perfectly, but the congressmen would not buy it. They did not want vote counting to be done quickly. Often the roll call was used for purposes of delay (filibustering).

This experience taught the young inventor a lesson. He decided to follow a simple rule: "First, be sure a thing is wanted or needed, then go ahead." By the time he died at 84, Edison had patented, singly or jointly, 1,093 inventions. Many were among the most useful and helpful inventions ever developed—including the motion-picture projector, the phonograph, and the incandescent electric lightbulb.

EARLY LIFE AND CAREER

Thomas Alva Edison was born in Milan, Ohio, on Feb. 11, 1847. His father, Samuel

Edison, was a freethinker who tried many different careers. His mother, Nancy Elliott Edison, was a schoolteacher. When Thomas was seven, the family moved to Port Huron, Mich. There he entered school and attended sporadically for five years. He was imaginative and inquisitive, but because much instruction was by rote and he had difficulty hearing, he was bored and was labeled a misfit. To compensate, he became an avid and omnivorous reader. By the time he was 12, he had also begun to do chemistry experiments and had his own laboratory in his father's basement.

When Edison was a teenager he became a telegraph operator. Telegraphy was one of the nation's most important communication systems at the time. Edison was good at sending and taking messages in Morse code. He loved tinkering with telegraphic instruments, and he developed several improvements for them. By early 1869 he had quit his telegraphy job to become a full-time inventor.

Edison moved to New York, bringing with him an idea for a stock quotation printing device. There he met Samuel Laws, who already had a stock printer in operation. When this machine broke down, Edison repaired it. He was then hired by Laws, and out of this association grew the development of a stock printer that worked perfectly. For this and other related inventions Edison expected to be paid only a few hundred dollars. He was shocked when Laws handed him a check for $40,000.

Edison used this money to start a laboratory and factory in Newark, N.J. He soon had 300 employees and began turning out a number of successful inventions. He had as many as 50 inventions at various stages of development and manufacture at one time. Most of these had to do with telegraphy.

Edison's work habits would strain his marriage with Mary Stillwell, a former employee of his laboratory. The couple wed in 1871 and had three children.

MENLO PARK

After five years in Newark, Edison opened a new laboratory and machine shop in Menlo Park, N.J. There, from 1876 to 1886, he did his finest work. He soon became world-famous as the Wizard of Menlo Park. Not all his inventions were made easily, however.

He worked on some for years and spent thousands of dollars in perfecting them. "Genius," he said, "is two percent inspiration and ninety-eight percent perspiration."

Edison's early work at Menlo Park centered on the telephone, which had been introduced by Alexander Graham Bell in 1876. The first Bell telephone was both a transmitter and a receiver. One spoke through it and then put it to one's ear to hear the reply. The instrument was also weak in reproducing the voice and picked up much static. Edison invented a carbon transmitter that greatly improved the telephone's sound capabilities. It was the standard design in telephone transmitters until the 1970s. He also invented a receiver that contained a button-sized chalk diaphragm.

THE PHONOGRAPH

Edison's telephone work led to his invention in 1877 of the first device that could record and reproduce sound—the phonograph. He called it a "talking machine." Edison's phonograph consisted of a revolving cylinder wrapped in tinfoil. A needle was pressed against the cylinder. Attached

Edison's success was due in part to his work habits. In the picture the inventor appears somewhat haggard at the close of five days and five nights of continuous work in perfecting the early wax-cylinder type of phonograph. U.S. Department of the Interior, National Park Service, Edison National Historic Site

to the needle were a diaphragm and a large mouthpiece.

When Edison spoke into the mouthpiece while rotating the cylinder, his voice made the diaphragm vibrate. This caused the needle to make indentations in the tinfoil. When a second needle traced over the indentations, the phonograph reproduced Edison's original words. When Edison first demonstrated the machine to his laboratory assistants, they were startled to hear coming from it the words, "Mary had a little lamb." For a time they thought Edison was playing a trick on them. Later, when everyone had become convinced of the reality of Edison's invention, he became world famous.

THE ELECTRIC LIGHTBULB

Edison next focused his efforts on producing an electric light to replace gas lighting. Although electric lighting had existed since the early 19th century, it was not yet practical for home use. Edison's aim was to invent a lamp that would become incandescent, or luminous, as a result of heat passing through it.

Edison made filaments, or threads, of many heat-resistant materials into glass globes. The heat crumbled the filaments into ashes. Later he pumped air out of the bulbs. Using platinum filaments in these vacuum bulbs, he had some success. But he needed an inexpensive substance to use for filaments. He continued his research for many months.

In October 1879 Edison introduced the modern age of light. In his laboratory he tensely watched a charred cotton thread glow for 40 hours in a vacuum bulb. He knew then that he had invented the first commercially practical incandescent electric light. In his continuing search for a filament that would work better than the cotton thread, carbonized bamboo seemed most successful. For nine years millions of Edison lamp bulbs were made with bamboo filaments. In time, however, the modern filament of drawn tungsten wire was developed.

Edison also devoted his energies to improving the dynamo to furnish the necessary power for electric lighting systems. In addition, he developed a complete system of distributing the current and built the first central power station in lower Manhattan in 1882.

To work on the power system, Edison moved his operations from Menlo Park to New York City. His wife died there in 1884. A widower with three young children, Edison married Mina Miller in 1886. They also had three children.

"INVENTION FACTORY" IN WEST ORANGE

In 1887 Edison opened a new laboratory in West Orange, N.J. He called it his "invention factory." The first major undertaking at the new laboratory was a return to the phonograph, which Edison had abandoned to work on electric lighting. Spurred by the work of competitors, Edison worked to create a phonograph that was practical for business and home use. In the 1890s he established facilities for the production of both phonographs and the records to play on them.

Meanwhile, in 1888, Edison and William K.L. Dickson had developed a motion-picture camera and a projector. The camera was called the Kinetograph. The projector, called the Kinetoscope, was a small box inside which the motion picture was projected.

The Kinetograph was an early motion-picture camera developed by Thomas A. Edison and William Dickson by 1890. U.S. Department of the Interior, National Park Service, Edison National Historic Site

The picture was viewed through a peephole, meaning that only one person at a time could view the show. Competitors soon developed projectors that displayed the pictures on a screen, which hurt the Kinetoscope's business. Edison then acquired a projector developed by Thomas Armat and marketed it under the name Vitascope.

On the laboratory grounds in 1893 Edison developed the first motion-picture studio. This was a tar-paper shack in West Orange that was called the "Black Maria." It was built on rails so that it could be moved around to take advantage of the sun as a scene was being filmed.

Another important product of the West Orange laboratory was the alkaline storage battery. By 1909, after a decade of work on the project, Edison was a principal supplier of batteries for submarines and electric vehicles.

LATER YEARS

During World War I Edison directed research into torpedo mechanisms and antisubmarine devices. In 1920, largely at his instigation, Congress established the Naval Research Laboratory, the first institution for military research.

In October 1929, 50 years after Edison had invented the incandescent lightbulb, the country paid tribute to him on Light's Golden Jubilee. The setting for the event was the new Edison Institute of Technology, established by Edison's friend Henry Ford in Dearborn, Mich. Here Ford moved the Menlo Park laboratory.

Edison died in West Orange on Oct. 18, 1931. His West Orange laboratory and his 23-room home, Glenmont, were designated a national historic site in 1955.

CHAPTER 22

NIKOLA TESLA

The brilliant inventor and electrical engineer Nikola Tesla developed the alternating current (AC) power system that provides electricity for homes and buildings. Tesla was granted more than 100 United States patents. Many of his discoveries led to electronic developments for which other scientists were honored.

Nikola Tesla was born in Smiljan, Cro., then part of Austria-Hungary, on July 9 or 10, 1856. He was often sick during his boyhood, but he was a bright student with a photographic memory. Against his father's wishes he chose a career in electrical engineering. After his graduation from the University of Prague in 1880, Tesla worked as a telephone engineer in Budapest, Hungary. By 1882 he had devised an AC power system to replace the weak direct current (DC) generators and motors then in use.

Tesla moved to the United States in 1884. Thomas Edison hired the young engineer as an assistant upon his arrival. Friction soon

Nikola Tesla. Science & Society Picture Library/Getty Images

developed between the two, and by 1886 Tesla had lost his job. In 1887 he received enough money from backers to build a laboratory of his own in New York City.

Tesla became a United States citizen in 1889. A year earlier he had received a patent for his AC power system. At the heart of this system was the efficient polyphase induction motor that he developed. George Westinghouse bought the patent rights from Tesla. Westinghouse then launched the campaign that established alternating current as the prime electrical power supply in the United States.

Tesla later invented a high-frequency transformer, called the Tesla coil, which made AC power transmission practical. He also experimented with radio and designed an electronic tube for use as the detector in a voice radio system almost 20 years before Lee De Forest developed a similar device. Tesla lectured before large audiences of scientists in the United States and Europe between the years 1891 and 1893.

Although Tesla had laid the theoretical basis for radio communication as early as 1892, Guglielmo Marconi claimed all basic radio patents because of his own pioneering work in the field. In 1915 Tesla made an unsuccessful attempt to obtain a court injunction against the claims of Marconi. When the United States Supreme Court reviewed this decision in 1943, however, it reversed the decision and invalidated Marconi's patents on the ground that they had indeed been anticipated by earlier work.

Tesla and Edison supposedly had been chosen to share a Nobel prize in physics. According to the report, Tesla declined his share of the award because of his doubt that Edison was a scientist in the strictest sense. Neither of them ever received the prize.

During his later years he led a secluded, eccentric, and often destitute life, nearly forgotten by the world he believed would someday honor him. Tesla died on Jan. 7, 1943, in New York City. The Tesla Museum in Belgrade, Ser., was dedicated to the inventor. In 1956 the tesla, a unit of magnetic flux density in the metric system, was named in his honor.

CHAPTER 23

HENRY FORD

In 1896 a horseless carriage chugged along the streets of Detroit, with crowds gathering whenever it appeared. Terrified horses ran at its approach. The police tried to curb this nuisance by forcing its driver, Henry Ford, to get a license. That car was the first of many millions produced by the automotive pioneer.

Henry Ford was born near Dearborn, Mich., on July 30, 1863. His mother died when he was 12. He helped on the family farm in summer and in winter attended a one-room school. Watches and clocks fascinated the boy. He went around the countryside doing repair work without pay, merely for the chance to tinker with machinery.

At 16 Ford walked to Detroit and apprenticed himself to a mechanic for $2.50 a week. His board was $3.50, so he worked four hours every night for a watchmaker for $2 a week. Later he worked in an

The winning Model T Ford entry pauses on a rutted road during the transcontinental race from New York City to Seattle in 1909. Courtesy of Ford Motor Company Archives

engine shop and set up steam engines used on farms. In 1884 he took charge of a farm his father gave him. He married and seemed settled down, but after two years he went back to Detroit and worked as night engineer for the Detroit Edison Company.

Ford built his first car in a little shed behind his home. It had a two-cylinder engine over the rear axle that developed four horsepower, a single seat fitted in a boxlike body, an electric bell for a horn, and a steering lever instead of a wheel. In 1899 Ford helped organize the Detroit Automobile Company, which built cars to order. Ford wanted to build in quantity at a price within the reach of many. His partners objected, and Ford withdrew.

In 1903 he organized the Ford Motor Company with only $28,000 raised in cash. This money came from 11 other stockholders. One investor put just $2,500 into Ford's venture (only $1,000 of it in cash). He drew more than $5,000,000 in dividends, and he received more than $30,000,000 when he sold all of his holdings to Ford in 1919.

Early automobile manufacturers merely bought automobile parts and assembled the cars. Ford's objective was to make every part that went into his cars. He acquired iron and coal mines, forests, mills, and factories to produce and shape his steel and alloys, his fuel, wood, glass, and leather. He built railroad and steamship lines and an airplane freight service in order to transport his products.

Mass production was Ford's main idea, and he replaced men with machines wherever possible. Each man was given only one task, which he did repeatedly until it became automatic. Conveyors brought the job to the man instead of having the man waste time going to the job. To cut shipping costs, parts were shipped from the main plants in the Detroit area and assembled into cars at branch plants.

Ford also won fame as a philanthropist and pacifist. He established an eight-hour day, a minimum wage of $5 daily (later raised to $6), and a five-day week. He built a hospital in Detroit with fixed rates for service and physicians and nurses on salary. He created the Edison Institute, which includes Greenfield Village and the Edison Institute Museum and trade schools. Independence Hall, Thomas Edison's early laboratory, and other famous old buildings were reproduced in the village, which is open to the public. During World War I Ford headed a party of pacifists to Norway in a failed attempt to end the war, but during both World War I and World War II his company was a major producer of war materials.

In 1945 Ford yielded the presidency of the company to his 28-year-old grandson, Henry Ford II. Ford died on April 7, 1947, at the age of 83. Most of his personal estate, valued at about $205,000,000, was left to the Ford Foundation, one of the world's largest public trusts.

CHAPTER 24

CHARLES MARTIN HALL

O n Feb. 23, 1886, a young man of 22 stood anxiously over a complicated mass of electric wires, crucibles, and heating apparatus in a woodshed in Oberlin, Ohio. For two hours Charles Martin Hall watched as the contents of one of the crucibles grew hotter and hotter. Finally, he turned off the powerful current and poured out the molten mass. Little silver-colored drops had separated and hardened into shining buttons of aluminum metal. Hall's discovery of the electrolytic method of aluminum production brought the metal into wide commercial use and became the foundation of aluminum production as we know it today. The problem was to find a mineral that melts at a low temperature and, when melted, dissolves aluminum oxide. Hall found the answer in cryolite.

Hall was born in Thompson, Ohio, on Dec. 6, 1863. Eight months after graduating from Oberlin College, he made his discovery. In April of the same year a Frenchman,

Charles Martin Hall. Science Source/Photo Researchers, Inc.

95

Paul-Louis-Toussaint Héroult, who had made the same discovery at almost the same time as Hall, was granted a French patent for the same process. Hall applied to the United States Patent Office in July 1886 for a patent for his discovery, but it was not granted until 1889.

At first Hall could not get financial backing. When production was under way, he was sued for stealing the Héroult process. Hall won the suit in 1893. He died on Dec. 27, 1914, in Daytona Beach, Fla.

CHAPTER 25

GEORGE WASHINGTON CARVER

American agricultural chemist George Washington Carver helped to modernize the agricultural economy of the South. He developed new products derived from peanuts and soybeans and promoted the planting of these legumes as a way of liberating the South from its dependency on cotton.

Carver was born a slave on a farm near Diamond Grove, Mo. Although he was freed after the American Civil War he lived until age 10 or 12 on his former owner's plantation, where he learned to draw and became interested in plants and animals. He then left and worked at a variety of jobs while he pursued an education. After earning his high school degree he attended Simpson College at Indianola, Iowa, and Iowa State College of Agriculture and Mechanic Arts (now Iowa State University) at Ames. At Iowa he earned a bachelor's degree in agricultural science in 1894 and a master's degree in 1896.

George Washington Carver. ©AP Images

Carver's achievements with plants brought him to the attention of Booker T. Washington, founder of the Tuskegee Normal and Industrial Institute (now Tuskegee University) in Alabama. Carver became head of Tuskegee's agriculture department in 1896. In his 47 years there the great plant scientist devoted his time to research projects aimed at helping Southern agriculture. He conducted experiments in soil management and crop production and directed an experimental farm. At this time agriculture in the Deep South was in serious trouble because the unremitting single-crop cultivation of cotton had left the soil of many fields exhausted and worthless, and erosion had then taken its toll on areas that could no longer sustain any plant cover. As a remedy, Carver urged Southern farmers to plant peanuts and soybeans, which, since they belong to the legume family, could restore nitrogen to the soil while providing the protein so badly needed in the diet of many Southerners. He ultimately developed some 300 derivative products from peanuts alone. When Carver first arrived at Tuskegee in 1896, the peanut had not even been recognized as a crop, but within the next half century it became one of the leading crops throughout the United States and, in the South, the second cash crop (after cotton) by 1940.

Carver was also a painter and a musician. In 1940 he used his life savings to establish the George Washington Carver Foundation for research in agricultural chemistry. During World War II he worked to replace the textile dyes formerly imported from Europe, and in all he produced dyes of 500 different shades. Ten years after his death in Tuskegee on Jan. 5, 1943, Carver's birthplace was dedicated as a national monument.

CHAPTER 26

THE WRIGHT BROTHERS

On a coastal sand dune near Kitty Hawk, N.C., on Dec. 17, 1903, two brothers, Orville and Wilbur Wright, realized one of mankind's earliest dreams: they flew. Although gliders were in existence, the Wright brothers made the world's first successful sustained and controlled flight of a motor-driven aircraft, the culmination of years of experimentation with kites and gliders.

Wilbur Wright was born near Millville, Ind., on April 16, 1867, and Orville in Dayton, Ohio, on Aug. 19, 1871. They were the sons of a clergyman who later became a bishop of the United Brethren Church. The boys demonstrated their mechanical abilities at an early age. A skating accident made Wilbur an invalid for several years. While in high school Orville built a printing press and started a weekly newspaper. The Wright brothers became inseparable, and neither married.

Wilbur (left) *and Orville Wright.* Science & Society Picture Library/Getty Images

In 1892 the brothers opened a bicycle sales and repair shop, and they were soon manufacturing their own bicycles. Even as young boys they were fascinated with flight, playing with kites and a toy helicopter. They became inspired by several glider pioneers, especially Otto Lilienthal in Germany and Octave Chanute in the United States. After observing how buzzards keep their balance while in the air, Wilbur realized that to fly successfully an airplane must operate on three axes.

In 1900 they built their first glider, a biplane, which traveled 300 feet (91 meters). In 1901, using aerodynamics tables compiled by Samuel Langley and Lilienthal, they constructed new wings for a larger glider; the flight was poor so they set out to test the tables. They made 200 model wings and tested them in a small wind tunnel. The tables were proven wrong and the Wrights painstakingly computed new ones. In 1902 their third biplane bested all records for glider flight.

To construct their first powered airplane, *Flyer I*, the Wrights had to design a lighter gasoline engine and an efficient propeller. In 1903, with a strong wind at Kitty Hawk, the Wrights tested the plane. Orville, the pilot, lay alongside the motor on the lower wing. Wilbur steadied the craft at one wing tip. After a 40-foot (12-meter) run the plane was airborne. In the 12 seconds before it touched the ground, the plane flew 120 feet (37 meters). Wilbur piloted the longest flight of the day, 852 feet (260 meters) in 59 seconds.

During 1904 and 1905 the Wrights built and tested new planes and engines. An improved *Flyer II* was flown near Dayton,

Ohio, in 1904. In 1905 the world's first practical airplane, Flyer III, could turn, bank, circle, fly figure eights, and stay airborne for over half an hour. Late in 1907, the Wrights submitted a bid to the United States Army for a military plane. In 1908 Orville took a plane to Fort Myer, Va., passed the trials, and won the contract for the world's first military plane. During that year, Orville's plane crashed, injuring him and killing his passenger.

Wilbur died of typhoid fever on May 30, 1912. Orville served on the National Advisory Committee for Aeronautics. For years he argued with officials of the Smithsonian Institution over whether the Wrights or Samuel Pierpont Langley had built the first successful plane. An angered Orville lent the Flyer I to the Kensington Museum in London in 1928. In 1942 Smithsonian officials made a public apology. Orville died in Dayton on Jan. 30, 1948. Later that year the plane was returned to the United States.

CHAPTER 27

GUGLIELMO MARCONI

The brilliant man who transformed an experiment into the practical invention of radio was Guglielmo Marconi. He shared the 1909 Nobel prize in physics for the development of wireless telegraphy.

Guglielmo Marconi was born on April 25, 1874, near Bologna, Italy. Even as a young boy Marconi was interested in science. He was particularly fascinated by physics, chemistry, and electricity. The boy was privately tutored and received his later scientific education at the University of Bologna.

In 1894 young Marconi read an obituary of Heinrich Hertz, the discoverer of Hertzian waves, which are now known as radio waves. The young man's imagination was stirred by the account given of Hertz's work, and the idea occurred to him that Hertzian waves might be used in communication. He set to work on apparatuses for sending and receiving telegraph

Guglielmo Marconi. Library of Congress Prints and Photographs Division

messages through the air and soon was able to transmit coded signals more than a mile. Marconi offered his invention to the Italian government, but it was rejected. In 1896 he went to England and took out a patent, the first ever granted for a practical system of wireless telegraphy. The next year a company was formed (later known as Marconi's Wireless Telegraph Company, Ltd.) to exploit wireless commercially. Its success made Marconi wealthy.

One of the first practical applications of wireless came in 1898, when Marconi followed the Kingstown Regatta in a tugboat and flashed the results in code to the offices of a Dublin newspaper. In 1899 the value of wireless telegraphy in saving lives at sea was first demonstrated. The East Goodwin Sands lightship was rammed in a fog, and aid was summoned by wireless.

In 1901 Marconi achieved a dramatic success when he transmitted signals across the Atlantic Ocean by wireless. Other scientists had thought this impossible, believing that radio waves traveled only in straight lines. Marconi, however, thought that the long waves he used would follow the curvature of the Earth. This was proved when, on Dec. 12, 1901, he received signals in St. John's, Newf., sent from a transmitter in Poldhu at the southwestern tip of England.

Marconi continued to improve his basic devices, sending messages farther and farther. In 1910 he was able to receive signals at Buenos Aires, Arg., from Clifden, Ire., and in 1918 he sent a message from England to Australia. Other scientists added their inventions such as the vacuum tube amplifier and the audion tube. By 1921 Marconi's wireless telegraphy had become wireless telephony, the voice radio of today.

As long-wave broadcasting became practical, Marconi turned his attention to short waves. By 1922 he had perfected the transmission of short waves by focusing the waves with a parabolic reflector behind the antenna. This system is employed now by most worldwide communications systems. Among his other useful inventions was the radio direction finder (RDF) by which ships and airplanes can fix their positions using radio signals. In 1934 Marconi demonstrated equipment that made instrument navigation of ships possible.

Another of Marconi's inventions, the autoalarm, picks up distress signals when radio operators are off duty and sounds a loud alarm. He was also a pioneer in the use of ultrahigh-frequency (UHF) waves for voice radio communication over short distances.

In 1929 Marconi was created a marchese (marquis). He lost the use of his right eye in an automobile accident in 1912. Politically Marconi was a Fascist, and until his death in Rome on July 20, 1937, he was in charge of scientific research under Benito Mussolini.

CHAPTER 28

LEE DE FOREST

Live radio broadcasting and transcontinental telephone calls were made possible by the Audion tube created by American inventor Lee De Forest. His invention ultimately helped bring radio and television to millions, yet he made almost no money from it.

Lee De Forest was born in Council Bluffs, Iowa, on Aug. 26, 1873. He became interested in science as a boy, and by the age of 13 he had invented several mechanical gadgets. A scholarship enabled him to attend the Sheffield Scientific School at Yale University. He earned a doctorate in physics at Yale in 1899.

After graduation he began working for the Western Electric Company, and he conducted his own experiments after hours. Although telegraph codes could be sent through the air by radio waves, no one had yet found a way to broadcast music or speech. While experimenting with John Ambrose Fleming's two-electrode vacuum tube, De Forest introduced a third electrode—a grid

Lee De Forest. Hulton Archive/Getty Images

between the filament and the plate. The grid controlled the flow of electrons through the tube, enabling it to amplify electrical signals. He patented this Audion tube in 1907 and broadcast a live Metropolitan Opera performance of Enrico Caruso in 1910. De Forest and others later realized that the Audion tube could also generate oscillating current and be used as a transmitter.

De Forest took out more than 300 patents for his inventions, including devices used in radio, telephones, television, and motion pictures. His Phonofilm system allowed motion picture sound tracks to be recorded on the film. In 1923 he used it to show the first public "talking" movie.

De Forest was not a savvy businessman, however, and he was twice defrauded by his business partners. He was also involved in more than 100 lawsuits regarding his patents. Discouraged and poorly advised, he sold the rights to the Audion tube and other inventions to telecommunications companies at very low prices. Wider recognition came to him in his later years, but he was bitter about the financial gains made by others on his inventions. He died on June 30, 1961, in Hollywood, Calif.

CHAPTER 29

NORA STANTON BLATCH BARNEY

Nora Stanton Blatch Barney was the first woman in the United States to obtain a degree in civil engineering as well as the first woman to be admitted as a member of the American Society of Civil Engineers (ASCE). She was also a noted suffragist leader and architect.

Nora Stanton Blatch was born on Sept. 30, 1883, in Basingstoke in Hampshire, Eng. She was the daughter of Harriot Stanton Blatch and the granddaughter of Elizabeth Cady Stanton, both of whom were leaders of the women's rights movement in the United States. After her family relocated to New York City, Blatch studied at Cornell University in Ithaca, New York, where she earned her civil engineering degree in 1905; the same year, she was admitted as a member (with junior status) of the ASCE. She worked for the American Bridge Company in 1905–06 and for the New York City Board of Water Supply. She also took courses in electricity and mathematics at Columbia University so that she could work as a laboratory assistant to Lee De Forest, whom she married in 1908. Blatch worked for her husband's company in New Jersey until 1909, when they were separated (they divorced in 1912).

After returning to New York City, Blatch worked as an assistant engineer and chief draftsman at the Radley Steel Construction Company (1909–12) and for several years

Nora Stanton Blatch Barney, 1921. National Photo Company Collection/Library of Congress, Washington, D.C.

as an assistant engineer for the New York Public Service Commission (from 1912). She began working part-time in 1914 as an architect and developer on Long Island. In 1916 she gained notoriety when she filed a lawsuit against the ASCE, which had terminated Blatch's membership when her age passed the limit for junior status; she failed to win reinstatement through the court.

In addition to her work in civil engineering, Blatch devoted her time to the woman suffrage movement. While studying at Cornell she had founded a suffrage club, and from 1909 to 1917 she campaigned heavily for the cause in New York. She became the president of the Women's Political Union in 1915, succeeding her mother, and edited the organization's *Women's Political World*. She subsequently participated in the efforts of the National Woman's Party for a federal Equal Rights Amendment.

In 1919 she married Morgan Barney, a marine architect. They moved to Greenwich, Conn., in 1923, and Nora Barney worked as a real estate developer. She remained politically active in her later years, writing such pamphlets as *Women as Human Beings* (1946). She died on Jan. 18, 1971, in Greenwich.

CONCLUSION

In the industrialized nations of the world, most of the products that people use today are turned out swiftly by the process of mass production, by people (and sometimes robots) working on assembly lines using power-driven machines. This modern mechanized system had its beginnings in the Industrial Revolution, the epochal period during which machines changed people's way of life as well as their methods of manufacture.

From England in the 18th century the Industrial Revolution spread gradually throughout Europe and thence to the United States and other parts of the world. This volume has covered the men and women responsible for many of the Industrial Revolution's most important technological changes. Among these breakthroughs were the use of new energy sources, the invention of new machines that increased production—including the steam engine and the spinning jenny—and the development of the factory system. There were great advances in communication as well; the telegraph, telephone, and radio made it possible to spread news rapidly over great distances. There were also tremendous developments in transportation, including the railroad, automobile, and airplane.

Economically, industrialization led to a wider distribution of wealth and increased international trade. Swift growth and change, however, brought problems as well as prosperity. In business some corporations became so large that they were able to squeeze out all rivals in their field. In the United States early government efforts to control these monopolies resulted in such legislation as the Interstate Commerce Act (1887) and the Sherman Anti-Trust Act (1890). In many countries, much attention was also focused on the plight of factory workers, whose working and living conditions were often very bad. Attempts to improve these conditions led to numerous strikes and ultimately gave rise to a widespread labor movement.

aerodynamics A branch of dynamics that deals with the motion of air and other gaseous fluids and with the forces acting on bodies in motion relative to such fluids.

audiometer An instrument used in measuring the acuity of hearing.

cotton gin A machine that separates the seeds, hulls, and foreign material from cotton.

cryolite A mineral consisting of a fluoride of sodium and aluminum found especially in Greenland usually in white cleavable masses and formerly used as a source of aluminum.

division of labor The breakdown of labor into its components and their distribution among different persons, groups, or machines to increase productive efficiency.

electrolytic Describing something produced by or used in electrolysis.

electromagnetism A fundamental physical force that is responsible for interactions between charged particles which occur because of their charge and for the emission and absorption of photons, that is about a hundredth the strength of the strong force, and that extends over infinite distances but is dominant over atomic and molecular distances.

electron An elementary particle consisting of a charge of negative electricity equal to about 1.602×10^{-19} coulomb and having a mass when at rest of about 9.109×10^{-31} kilogram or about 1/1836 that of a proton.

horsepower A unit of power equal in the United States to 746 watts and nearly equivalent to the English gravitational unit of the same name that equals 550 foot-pounds of work per second.

industrialist One owning or engaged in the management of an industry.

lockstitch A sewing machine stitch formed by the looping together of two threads one on each side of the material being sewn.

locomotive A self-propelled vehicle that runs on rails and is used for moving railroad cars.

mechanical engineering A branch of engineering concerned primarily with the industrial application of mechanics and with the production of tools, machinery, and their products.

monopoly Exclusive ownership through legal privilege, command of supply, or concerted action.

Nobel Prize Any of various annual prizes (as in peace, literature, medicine) established by the will of Alfred Nobel for the encouragement of persons who work for the interests of humanity.

pacifist Someone who is strongly and actively opposed to conflict and especially war.

patent A writing securing for a term of years the exclusive right to make, use, or sell an invention.

philanthropist One who makes an active effort to promote human welfare.

pioneer A person or group that originates or helps open up a new line of thought or activity or a new method or technical development.

prolific Marked by abundant inventiveness or productivity.

reaper Any of various machines for cutting grain.

scythe An implement used for mowing (as grass) and composed of a long curving blade fastened at an angle to a long handle.

suffragist One who advocates extension of suffrage, especially to women.

telegraph An apparatus for communication at a distance by coded signals.

transformer A device employing the principle of mutual induction to convert variations of current in a primary circuit into variations of voltage and current in a secondary circuit.

trust A combination of firms or corporations formed by a legal agreement.

vulcanization The process of treating crude or synthetic rubber or similar plastic material chemically to give it useful properties (as elasticity, strength, and stability).

FOR MORE INFORMATION

MIT Museum
Building N51
265 Massachusetts Avenue
Cambridge, Ma 02139
(617) 253-5927
Web site: web.mit.edu/museum
The MIT Museum, part of the
    Massachusetts Institute of Technology,
    spotlights some of the most innovative
    scientific and technological developments
    of the past, present, and future, putting
    into perspective the pioneering work
    done by those profiled in this book.

Museum of Science and Industry
57th Street and Lake Shore Drive
Chicago, IL 60637
(773) 684-1414
Web site: www.msichicago.org
The Museum of Science and Industry is the
    largest science center in the Western
    Hemisphere, according to its Web site.
    The museum offers the public a variety
    of exhibits that display the convergence
    of science and its application to the
    industrial world.

Nikola Tesla Museum
Krunska 51, Belgrade, Serbia
+ 381 11 24 33 886
Web site: http://www.tesla-museum.org/
meni_en.htm
The Nikola Tesla Museum was founded in
1952 and aims to preserve the heritage of
this great innovator, including thousands
of his documents, books, journals,
photographs, and drawings.

Wright Brothers National Memorial
1401 National Park Drive
Manteo, North Carolina 27954
(252) 441-7430
Web site: www.nps.gov/wrbr
The Wright Brothers National Memorial
is located in the Outer Banks of North
Carolina, where these pioneers made
aviation history.

WEB SITES

Due to the changing nature of Internet links,
Rosen Publishing has developed an online
list of Web sites related to the subject of this
book. This site is updated regularly. Please
use this link to access the list:

http://rosenlinks.com/inven/indupi

FOR FURTHER READING

Adair, Gene. *Thomas Alva Edison: Inventing the Electric Age* (Oxford Univ. Press, 1996).

Bagley, Katie. *Eli Whitney: American Inventor* (Bridgestone Books, 2003).

Buckley, Susan Washburn. *The Industrial Revolution: 1790–1850* (National Geographic Society, 2002).

Burgan, Michael. *Henry Ford* (World Almanac Library, 2002).

Corrick, James A. *The Industrial Revolution* (Lucent Books, 1998).

Jenner, Caryn. *First Flight: The Story of the Wright Brothers* (DK Publishing, 2003).

McCormick, Anita Louise. *The Industrial Revolution in American History* (Enslow Publishers, 1998).

Rider, Christine, ed. *Encyclopedia of the Age of the Industrial Revolution, 1700–1920* (Greenwood Press, 2007).

Sakolsky, Josh, ed. *Critical Perspectives on the Industrial Revolution* (Rosen Publishing Group, 2005).

Samuels, Charlie. *Timeline of the Industrial Revolution* (Gareth Stevens, 2010).

Smith, Nigel. *The Industrial Revolution* (Raintree Steck-Vaughn Publishers, 2003).

INDEX